PEDRO THE ROMAN DONKEY

Written by

David Jamilly

Creative input: Felix Amedoda

Illustrations by Graham Evans

Nightingale Books

Pedro is the greatest donkey the world has ever known.

Pedro is a young hardworking Roman donkey...

... who is also very creative.

He invented many things like dustbin vans and aeroplanes (he calls them metal birds).

But he is also very sensitive.

Once he was so upset by a rude man that...

...he left Rome and went to Leamington Spa...

...and then to the seaside.

His favourite meal is sandwiches with soda water.

And he loves soft music.

Pedro has lots of special friends like Sam and Sara and Sadia.

He also invented spaceships and submarines.

And is now building a sanctuary for hardworking donkeys.

Pedro is a very creative and sensitive donkey.

Pedro is the greatest donkey the world has ever known.

NIGHTINGALE PAPERBACK

© Copyright 2021
David Jamilly

The right of David Jamilly to be identified as author of
this work has been asserted by him in accordance with the
Copyright, Designs and Patents Act 1988.

All Rights Reserved

No reproduction, copy or transmission of this publication
may be made without written permission.
No paragraph of this publication may be reproduced,
copied or transmitted save with the written permission of the publisher, or in
accordance with the provisions
of the Copyright Act 1956 (as amended).

Any person who commits any unauthorised act in relation to
this publication may be liable to criminal
prosecution and civil claims for damages.

A CIP catalogue record for this title is
available from the British Library.

ISBN 978-1-83875-233-0

*Nightingale Books is an imprint of
Pegasus Elliot MacKenzie Publishers Ltd.
www.pegasuspublishers.com*

First Published in 2021

**Nightingale Books
Sheraton House Castle Park
Cambridge England**

Printed & Bound in Great Britain

www.ingramcontent.com/pod-product-compliance
Lightning Source LLC
LaVergne TN
LVHW072013060526
838200LV00059B/4671